The Trouble with a Short Horse in Montana

The Trouble with a Short Horse in Montana

poems

Roy Bentley

White Pine Press / Buffalo, New York

White Pine Press,
P.O. Box 236, Buffalo, NY 14201 www.whitepine.org

Acknowledgments: *American Literary Review:* "What Keats' Motives Were in Studying Medicine Are Not Known with Any Certainty" and "Hard Rain after Drought"; *Artful Dodge*: "Row Houses," "The Beasts of the Fields," "Speaking with a Single Tongue," "Shooting Water Buffalo near An Loc," "History," "Detail from the Bombing of a Thing Struck by Light," "Jerry Lee Lewis at the Gates to Graceland," and "Unfit"; *The Danforth Review*: "Conscripted"; *Grand Valley Review*: "Wild Turkeys, First Light"; *Green Mountains Review*: "All This and Hell to Look Forward to"; *The Journal*: "The Morning After the Running of the 116th Kentucky Derby," sections 4, 5, 11 & 12 of "The Trouble with a Short Horse in Montana," "Red Scarf," "My Hands Enter Dirt Easily, a Premonition"; *Mid-American Review*: "The Bodies of Bees"; *North American Review*: "Motorcade"; *The Ohio Review*: "The Heron Tattoo"; *Pleiades*: "Air Freight"; *Prairie Schooner*: "The Other Pile" and "The Beautiful Bird Revealing the Unknown to a Pair of Lovers"; *Riverwind*: "The Wreck of the Barbie Ferrari," "Rocket Man," "The Captain's Driver," "Light as Story" and "Appalachian Cooking for Two"; *Rosebud*: "Because If Things Are Not Carefully Hidden"; *Shenandoah*: "The Gratitude of Snakes"; *Southern Review*: "Why Palestinian Men Fire Submachine Guns in the Direction of the Bone-colored Face of the Man in the Moon," "The Whore Is Born in Texas," "News of God" and "The Politics of Spit"; *Three Plum Review*: "Adult Films".

"On the Way to a Bob Dylan Concert" and "Second-billed to Simon & Garfunkel at Forest Hills, New York, Jim Morrison Faces a Disinterested Audience" were included in the anthology *Three Cord Poems: the Poetry of Rock 'n Roll* published by deepcleveland press. "The Wreck of the Barbie Ferrari" was reprinted in the anthology *Hymns to the Outrageous* published by Pudding House Publications.

Two chapbooks—*Reparation* and *Greatest Hits: 1982-2001*—were assembled from the contents of this collection. My thanks to Jennifer Bosveld, series editor for Pudding House.

Certain poems in Part I owe a debt of gratitude to Larry Reilly, a friend, who served in Vietnam at the height of the war. (My service was stateside, and from 1972 to 1974.)

I wish to thank both the Ohio Arts Council and the National Endowment for the Arts for Individual Artist Fellowship awards in poetry received during the writing of this book.

The White Pine Press Poetry Prize, Volume Number 11

First Edition

10-digit ISBN 1-893-996-77-8
13-digit ISBN 978-1-893996-77-9

Printed and bound in the United States of America

Library of Congress Control Number: 2006923281

for Gloria

Contents

— One —

The Politics of Spit / 11
Conscripted / 12
The Basic Training Poem / 13
The Whore Is Born in Texas / 15
News of God / 17
Rocket Man / 19
History / 20
The Captain's Driver / 21
Detail from the Bombing of a Thing Struck by Light / 22
Vietnamese Boy Offers Found Purple Heart for Food / 23
The Power of Intelligent Engineering:
The P-38 Can Opener / 24
Shooting Water Buffalo near An Loc / 25
The Gratitude of Snakes / 26
Unfit / 27
Why Palestinian Men Fire Submachine Guns in the Direction
of the Bone-colored Face of the Man in the Moon / 28

— Two —

The Trouble with a Short Horse in Montana / 31

— Three —

What Keats' Motives Were in Studying Medicine
Are Not Known with Any Certainty / 47
Shelley, after the Fatigue of an Unusually Long Walk / 49
The Beautiful Bird Revealing the Unknown
to a Pair of Lovers / 50
Wild Turkeys, First Light / 51

The Heron Tattoo / 52
Because If Things Are Not Carefully Hidden / 53
The Wreck of the Barbie Ferrari / 54
Shaved and Confused or Why a Woman Who Made Lord Byron
a Gift of Her Pubic Hair Was Jealous of His Gift
of £500 to Lady Falkland / 56
Hard Rain after Drought / 57
Elvis on a Surfboard / 58
Jerry Lee Lewis at the Gates to Graceland / 59
Adult Films / 61
Second-billed to Simon & Garfunkel at Forest Hills,
Jim Morrison Faces a Disinterested Audience / 62
The Bodies of Bees / 63
On the Way to a Bob Dylan Concert / 64

— Four —

Motorcade / 67
Roy's Shell, 1962 / 69
Hillbilly Music / 70
Speaking with a Single Tongue / 72
The Morning After the Running
of the 116th Kentucky Derby / 77
Row Houses / 78
Light as Story / 80
My Name Is Bentley / 81
Appalachian Cooking for Two / 83
My Hands Enter Dirt Easily, a Premonition / 84
The Beasts of the Fields / 85
Red Scarf / 86
Kitchen / 87
Air Freight / 89
All This and Hell to Look Forward to / 90
The Other Pile / 92

One

The Politics of Spit

Without our uniforms, the haircuts
betray everything: we're *servicemen*
and enlistees since no one gets drafted
into the Air Force, which makes us doubly
hated in Champaign, Illinois in 1973.
It's the Ray-Bans and white-sidewall, trimmed-
around-the-ears hairlength in the Age
of Aquarius. Still, I'm stunned when someone
lets go a huge you-know that lands at our
feet then a smaller one that hits me
like the realization America isn't one country.
We're just standing there, stupefied, checking
ourselves like the ones in the Real War
must have had to after a fire fight. A command
to oneself not to fold, not here, little coins
of cruelty abloom on this broadcloth shirt.
It is when I stand like this—
shamed, changed forever, past the splatter,
that I feel what it is to be taken in
by an idea of one's own worthiness,
to die to that and learn about the nature
of Power and its companion Humiliation.
I think this stuff soaks in, and it does.
Marked this way, I can begin.

Conscripted

The day my father was to go to the barber
I went into the basement, under the stairs,
hid behind boxes of Christmas decorations
stacked on cases of Mason jars of jellies,
my father's mothballed Army uniforms,
and prayed not to be found and have to go.
I had every intention, in 1971, of letting
my hair grow over the ears and collar—
a mop-top Beatle cut, at the very least,
but he must have known where to look
or knew it was that important. I think
I had given up on his America, on trying
to grow up to be the Good Son, and I know
I wanted to get stoned on a matchbox-sized
nickel bag of marijuana. I was 17, and
there was the Draft and Vietnam between us,
and so we fought right there, in the basement.
I could not imagine besting him, mostly
I was him, in altered form, conscripted,
but at least for a long moment no scissors
subtracted from my dream of a man. I heard
get going, goddammit, no son of mine as he
shoved me up the stairs and out the door. And
when we got to the shop, we were still at it.
Winning by force and shouting, he called me
a shit, in a voice that roared like machinery
until the barber, a friend of his, said "Play it
cool, Roy." (The barber used the name Roy, also
my father's name, but I knew he meant me.) He
looked around his shop, at the crowd of men, said
it was, after all, just a haircut and couldn't hurt—
not worth the fuss, nothing to come to blows over.

The Basic Training Poem

It was when the sergeants had gone home
and those airmen (corporals) they left in charge
said that if we wouldn't say anything
they wouldn't and let those of us in Casual Status
—which meant we'd been released out of
the regular rotation of basic training and put
on hold, as it were, for drugs or being queer
or wetting the bed, whatever—go into town.
San Antonio, Texas. We wore "civvies"
—civilian clothes—and took a bus to the Alamo
like the tourists we were, watching the Texans
give the finger to the Mexicans all over again,
and vice versa, everywhere you went. I went
to a movie theater where I sat so quietly,
in the dark, that people kept stepping on me.
Watched the same George C. Scott movie I'd seen
back home in Ohio, the one where he's Patton
and punches some private (slaps him) publicly.
Gets himself relieved of command, for a slap.
It was October, still warm, and I went to a theater
for the air conditioning and darkness. I'd confessed
to having taken LSD and been shipped off to Casual,
then told the people in Casual I'd lied because I was
homesick. They bought it, slapped me on the back.
Told me which of the other airmen to steer clear of.
They gave me extra liberty, hinted they'd done worse
and, what the hell, we were in Texas. They said
I should get drunk on Lone Star beer, get laid. Sit tight.
They said they'd get me back into basic training. So
I watched George C. Scott every night for a month.
At the Alamo Cineplex. Outside, in San Antonio,
highschoolers in jacked-up Novas and Chevelles

flipped the finger to 1972. I hated George C. Scott,
Casual Status, the airmen who gave me the passes.
I wanted to be somewhere else, wanted to give the finger
to my life thus far. But I sat in the dark, hour after hour,
chilled and alone, waiting to get back in. Then
I would walk down streets of adobed storefronts,
dreaming that there was a better movie house
than the one I kept wandering into, out of.
There were buses, but I had all this time to kill.
I'd walk the miles back to base, rain or shine,
and I'd wave to the Texans who flipped me off.
To the Mexicans who looked like they'd been slapped.
I'd wave in the direction of the Alamo Cineplex,
that same shrine of a movie they never changed.

The Whore Is Born in Texas

It starts with the butts we're field-stripping
in a rolling motion between thumb and index finger,
tobacco and filter floss scattered
in no special direction onto flat squadron lawns.
Someone's told us to police the area.

The first black guy I've spoken to in my life
wants to talk, says he's from Detroit.
The next step is mine: *I've taken LSD*
at least twenty times, but I can't get laid.
There's no premeditation to it, no scheming;

this is everything true I know to say.
He says, You're a damn holy man.
He's got a big gap-toothed smile, looks
like a short Malcolm X in Air Force fatigues.
(I've read about Malcolm in *Life* magazine.)

It starts to rain, big drops, and he tells me
if we ever get leave he'll show me
a place in town, all the tricks. We're
getting soaked, more so by the minute.
He says his name's Leonard, but

that I should call him Butch. Says
he'll call me Whore in the same way
they call big men Tiny. I like him.
You smoke? I ask. There's that no-apologies
smile you can buy whatever you need with.

I don't think: *Gee, we're going to be friends.*
I think this broad, flat nose a very perfect bird's
wing, his expression that of a kid playing hooky.
Not cigarettes, he says, letting go leaf
into that other life of west Texas wind.

News of God

Pre-dawn, late February. Lines of uniforms and
the voices of boots, base streets a second flesh
of ice. There's little to do this early
but half-step and pray. He's short, Butch,
in the rear of the column, says later that he

sees me falling to earth, disappearing abruptly
up ahead in the blue dark. This night
is ice for miles running, and it's forcing
big men and small to call out *Christ Jesus*
and reach for whomever's at hand. Or nothing.

I can see the glare as off of a lake
whose still surface receives the weight of men.
It's like a movie, guys in snaking lines
making a hole for the fallen. Say you've
fallen, sit amazed, and no one will stop. No one.

Suddenly, the dark behind those on the road
opens to extend a merciful hand and *Wham*—
you both go down. Say you're both laughing now,
or else you're about to, and this hand's
still holding on. You want it to release

but you need it. The thing is you can't, finally,
go on without help. Something else: you fall,
rise, fall, and keep giving orders to God
or Heaven concerning the disposition
of all this ice, the indifferent season,

a shiny-with-starlight state of Texas
that has turned a kind of silver underfoot.
In that moment the air itself parts, yields.
It knows something about keeping its balance, about
distances traveled in a whole other country.

Rocket Man

He says "mortars sing." Points at his stockpile,
calls the rounds Singers then draws a bayonet
and stirs the coffee in his canteen cup.
The dark clock of cup clicks; somebody
coughs in the first light. A night ago,
on perimeter watch, small rustling sounds
were the "wings of angels" he could "touch"
from a distance. It isn't easy, being here.

We are the first ones up this morning,
and we know the gooks are winning
because Hanoi Jane Fonda says so in *Time.*
Beyond the line of claymores, the earth relaxes.
Can you hear the stiff latch of a safety
being clicked back on? I can't.
I can't hear shit as a Huey, farther off,
studies the huge green of terrain, sucks air.

He gets this way this morning, talking to be talking,
to reabsorb all those cocked hours on watch
that stretch everlastingly into more than one night.
I can't say anything beyond *Smoke this, cowboy.*
My own tiredness rises like a chopper, singing
to the dead air as it passes in and
through the shadow that nothing makes.

History

When the other guy in the truck says *This sucks,*
he's not talking about the light on banyan leaves
nor is he talking about the string of village girls
pouring from hooches for the chance to perform

fellatio for two one-dollar bills, American cigarettes.
When the other guy in the truck lights up,
the smoke says it's opium and, truly,
today you're glad to have it offered. White wings

of the smoke fill with rain sounds, the convoy
recommencing its errand. How shrill the gears
that seem not to know what to make of this deep
utterance of tires on clay, the bass grind

of again beating the odds along for the ride.
This doesn't suck, you say, handing back across
the doctored Marlboro, something like a huge load
all in place and starting to be moved.

The Captain's Driver

The pneumatic wiper's *zish-zish* can't touch the drops
that run down the inside of the Jeep's windshield.
You're no inflatable driver, talking
incessantly the whole way to Saigon.
The captain says, *Just get us there, Reilly.*
Removes the silver bars signifying rank, pockets them.

The age of the air, the hour of one star
are the stuff you miss this morning
pulling up in front of the Pleasure Zone.
My treat, Private the captain says when you're parked
in front of a house whose history is wood, other summers.

You get out, circle the Jeep in the rain
to intercept the captain. A boy splashes in a puddle
the color of the city this morning; he says
something to you then the captain, in Vietnamese,
about a need for chocolate. Inside, it's the same—

Pick me, G.I.—all the weary brown eyes on you
that aren't on the captain. Plains Indians back home
call this month the Moon of Most Heat. You'd
know this had you listened to what you slept through.
Later, you'll say you slept through even this.

Detail from the Bombing of a Thing Struck by Light

What I remember of Saigon, besides Tu Do Street,
is how a silk sunflower top blossomed
one afternoon in a glass snifter in the wreckage
of a shop Victor Charlie had spared until Tet—
the flower was this smaller explosion
that iridesced as it caught the light.

Sure, hell, it was tacky—too much, and fake:
whoever heard of sunflowers in the Mekong delta?

But after they blew the place up, leveled it
and then some, I shuddered with pleasure
when I thought of that flower "floating"—
just sitting there, guarding the brightnesses
of even this world where, with every breath I took,
less of me breathed what was good in us.

Vietnamese Boy Offers Found Purple Heart for Food

The rhetoric of American supremacy
has fallen among bomb-collapsed huts
and ghosts the dirt road he walks,
pausing here and there to dig at something
that shines in spite of itself.

Wrenching it free of 1973, he liberates
a box of memories from republican rubble.
The contents of the box he knows like a face
before it belongs to photographs
and cemeteries and the sound of wind.

For better or worse, the weather of war
has made him think he is one of them
and deserving of a decoration. Not
for honor but for moving in territories
that have become fleshed with regret.

And the ordinary light of afternoon
is correcting the boy again, making
of the blackened thatch of roofs
the universal sign for want. That sign
then fills the jungle air. Nothing

to be done but to fall in with others
who sweep toward trucks and APCs.
Ration tins and a handful of Hershey bars
cancel an anthem of exhaust.
The line for mercy is unconscionably long.

The Power of Intelligent Engineering: The P-38 Can Opener

Whatever requisite shit hole you collapse in,
whatever dream of doom you wake from,
there comes that rolling in the stomach
when the animal wants fed, finally,
no matter whose god you promised what
to keep you in one piece in this country.
Nothing is redeemed in the inexorable fact
of hungering, and here is a key: a tooth
sharp as moonlight, tiny bayonet edge,
able to pierce and track the lip of whatever:
the unmistakable tool of just getting by.
Here's where it begins, it says. Where it ends.

Shooting Water Buffalo near An Loc

I squeeze the naked, oil-smelling M-60,
direct a huge booming. For the hell of it.
A beautiful tangent of gray meat, below,

looks up at the known sky's new churning.
This afternoon, we're LBJ's big stick
and cheer the hammered beast's kicking,

shoulder clefts shimmering pink as roses
as it goes over—hacked, convulsing:
a shadow on the whipped up water.

The Cobra is a dark bird whose world
boils with matters of life and death. Better
to take for granted rightness than ask

who deserves what by which set of hands
and how much miracle or think what lets
this warm floor shudder with rising.

The Gratitude of Snakes

You had to feed the thing a rat.
And often it wouldn't get anywhere near
That rat, for reasons known
Only to snakes. Instead,

While the rat huddled, watching,
The snake struck thick aquarium glass
Or your exposed hand—

To remind you what was wild in that room.

You got bit, careful or not, and it stung.
Ask Ralph Hupp: I wouldn't call what happened
To his face a kiss of thanks. Nothing

Like the old antagonisms rising in an air
Of pure surprise. Nothing like
A man tugging at the snake on his face,
The snake on his face holding on

As if they were, together, snake and man,
One mouth trying to swallow. You know
A big, pained *God Almighty* went out.

And from the two sets of eyes—
Seeing as for the first time—
That same light that always escapes.

Unfit

Where I went, after they were through
taking back the uniforms, breaking my heart,
was to Ohio, my parents' home,
with the crisp October air to soften
all that disgrace, the overarching sycamores
of the better-of-two roads into town
dusting me with leaf-scent and sun and a lack of gloom

and dropping palm-sized tokens onto the shoulders
of pedestrians, hero and outlier alike, raining
down a golden message: you can outlast anything.
My father said: *You've shamed us.* Everyone else
was weary of talk of war and the calamity
of Southeast Asia. There was sufficient shame
to go around; the pallbearers of another America

buried the best of themselves, went back to work
walking stiffly toward ruined futures. Loss builds,
by definition, as monument every day. I took
a job bending pipe until the blood raced again.
The ache of being futureless was freeing; I worked
16-hour shifts, all the overtime they'd give me,
until they laid the whole lot of us off that Christmas.

They said: *We've got enough pipe for now. Happy
Holidays.* And snow fell in wet-heavy handfuls
through sycamores wanting nothing, wishless,
or wanting only to be what they were, unbowed.
There's just so much bending you can do, it turns out.
As if anyone could be found fit for his life, could bend
to fit this life; fill it like a suit of clothes, or uniform.

Why Palestinian Men Fire Submachine Guns in the Direction of the Bone-colored Face of the Man in the Moon

They have forgotten physics and the *Qur'an*
of gravity. Bullets go up like prayers; a sky and
faint stars concede only that there are rules to this.
It's nightfall; barrel flashes light the storefronts
and stone streets of Bethlehem. Sometimes
peace is an absolution of little thunders by a shop
that can't keep posters of Clint Eastwood in stock.
Sometimes the sun sets like the end of a western.

Even now, a soccer star's fugitive brother
sleeps in a different neighbor's house each night
to avoid arrest, re-imprisonment. Sometimes
he dreams of his 46-year-old mother in a hospital,
dying alone, compassion the property of those
who can call down God as border guards. Tonight,
a radio of explosives on a shoulder hails a taxi.
Oh, turn it up, someone says. *American music.*

Two

The Trouble with a Short Horse in Montana

I.

Your father is sitting with friends
at 3 A.M. in a Howard Johnson's,
watching a wall of white brick accept the cold.
Someone else from the closing air base
says, *Who said the Cold War is over?*
There are doughnuts and a German chocolate cake
pedestaled on a counter of Formica and chrome
and a glass pot of coffee on a warmer.
A cook slides a plate of eggs and toast
through the smoke of endless low-tar cigarettes.
A waitress figures tax and pretends
not to listen to arguments for and against
Joe Montana being God Almighty. Outside,
the four lanes of the state route steam
with a salting of snow going up whole.
The brute voices of truck engines sound, busted-hearted,
the pumplights out at the Texaco station, the still block
the small brilliances of business signs. The eyes
of the waitress fill with one November night.
She could smile at your father but it wouldn't help.

2.

It's his weekend and I'm free to roam
the lot and lift-bays of his service station.
There is a woman in a wedding dress at the pumps
and the white numbers click incrementally.
The fueling hose is back on the hook:
something from the dripping nozzle goes up
like any heady kitchen scent—bread
or gingerbread or pinto beans simmering all day.
There are pyramids of cans that point to a great need
broad and thick as bearing grease or oil leavings
on the floor of the bay where they come
to be made new or good as new.
There's a stock room where hydraulic hissings
compress the hour, impossibly, into a hand—
I sleep through the late-night raisings and lowerings
that begin each overhaul under the hum of electric light.
Finally, I sleep through the song of the pump bell.
They say the Hubble telescope has recorded Creation's holy shine
riding the bang of the first gaseous instants. I'm waiting
for the thread-scripted *Roy* on the pocket of a uniform.

3.

I had come prepared to watch Gene Autry
vault onto Champion and ride through fire.
Gene could have strummed "Tumbling Tumbleweeds."
But he arrived late; it rained. Now I see us
ushered from the grandstand into lines
to a tent where the air stank instantly
of horse shit. This wasn't my dream of America.
One kid, getting soaked, said, *This ain't Trigger.*
I didn't say anything. The rain had doused
the infield; rain ran into my cowboy boots.
But, inside the tent, Gene Autry got up
on the back of his famous horse. Said
we could, too. And I took a turn, six years old
and frightened to death of horses.
There were cowboys and cowgirls, a tentful
from all over Montgomery County, Ohio. Unmoored,
tent sides flapped and rose like the skirt of that other movie star.
Whatever else I have, Gene Autry is all smiles.
There was, or there wasn't, another ride.

4.

When you consider the scrap biscuits, the act itself
of apportioning what's at hand and the flouring pat
and reforming of what might have been one thing, loaves,
but will do quite nicely, thank you, as this other—
when you consider that an ancient wrist at forehead
brushing back the errant strand of hair pauses
and that nothing else is lost in pausing; when you
consider the absolute abundance of inner resource
in the face of one so accustomed to sighing, that a face
is as much light as anything; when you consider
the thousand failures of heart absorbed by the blood,
that such a multitude of disappointments becomes a self
and fuels the unillumined in us in the way a stubborn fire catches;
when you consider the *O* of the mouth shaping its own
new sound and phoneme for *You can't win,* that noise
of that sort is exactly what mercy should fly to
like a mother to a newborn's loud testimony to want;
when you consider how absence wracks a body
regardless of size or shape or age, that it is to suckle
we want and not be turned away, then

5.

we hear the cry of the believer-fallen-from-belief
as beginning and not the final word on God
or our lives in the light and the other work of hearts,
which is the bread we expect like the next sun, the next,
and we are permitted only so much joy for the reason
that we would stand and feast and crowd the table,
though the rest starved and went to bed hungry, wincing
at the inequalities God is maker of, and because saying
and singing for our place at the feast would pass away,
lift and fall, like the breasts of this one so broken
and yet breaking off her grief in the way weather changes.
Suddenly I am listening to what it means to be here.
All night there has been talk of demons and sin
and Myrtle, my aunt Myrtle, has prayed and sang
but now this morning she is up making biscuits.
Flour rises in bright divinations on the wind of her motion,
of her working out her rage at the death of my uncle,
even that become something extra for a child up early
who watches as if hungry for something besides bread, though
bread should be religion enough, Eucharist and resurrection.

6.

Because all one summer I prayed to fly—
first in the orchard, and always on a branch
when I loved the dirt as much as any kid
apprenticed to aloneness, a journeyman at 9
graduated to talking aloud to himself or singing
those songs of love the transistor resonated with.
Just an idea, as they say. Then I began to ask
and imagine an itching as with new skin—
now and again the random leaping of faith, groundward,
from high enough up I could have been killed
but wasn't, which led to more praying and falling
because I believed I kept company with God Himself.
I blame the orchard. It was too beautiful, too
quiet—a kind of house of monastic bliss boys crave
like the neighbor girl's breasts. I filled it with prayer
of a lion-hearted sort, as in *Hey, you, Old Man.*
It hardly matters now. It so happens
I got my fill of bruised fruit and getting
bruised myself; it was expensive, believing,
but I fooled that place in the brain flashes DANGER

7.

another, clearer voice telling me to forget it, forget
all about wings. After so long, you see your impression
in the grasses and get the idea. I got it.
I saw that I was alone in the orchard.
I saw that the only wings I was sprouting
were the raised places where rock had found flesh
and flesh had grown angelic all right—wings of dislocations,
pairs of bruises blue as summer sky, yellow sprains,
black-yellow like a June apple gone at the core.
And sore—I couldn't walk without suffering again
each failure, each unanswered asking. I felt
God's great deafness with every step. I *believed*—
but you learn. I knew the real and present pain
of there being nothing and no one to catch you. I knew
the only hand that would break my fall banged limbs
unmercifully all the way down. Then
I was still moving, still alive; I had flown
all we ever fly on faith. I saw the weight
of the body was mine to cart around a while.
I wear the rock-scars, I can tell you.

8.

A taxi, Chevy engine as voice, that voice
of dead metals shushed in the 6 A.M. fog,
from either white door of the taxi the hand-
lacquered word GLORY leaping out at you,
blue-black, blooming in the ordinary morning air.
If you were thirty-nine, say forty,
and had escaped a bad marriage for a few days
of friendship with a woman, you might
wake early, unwilling to sleep soundly
in the wide bed of a not-so-bad hotel room.
You might rise, as I did, dress quietly,
and go about in the fine chill of early March
to think life all right again or pretty good.
You might watch street traffic, patient as stone,
so that when the light called to you, like this,
with a single word signifying victory
or recognition after long trial, some sure sign,
you were there to receive it. Nothing more.
There is a world, after all, wants what you want.
The triumph, a fierce heart. Nothing less.

9.

I think of my pregnant, just-deserted mother
smoking a cigarette, sitting on a sofa
dissolved now into memory, the power off
and the house dark, all the clocks hushed and
showing the hour and minute after which
nothing moved ever again because someone
loved us. We can't write ourselves
out of our unhappier times. I'm there,
a presence; I do not have to imagine it.
So much of loss is what lives with us
after what lived with us is gone. I'll see,
always, her rising to walk the cold linoleum,
the lights in the other houses coming on
in the living room's black tiles. I do not
ask for mercy for myself in this life—
only the heart the body uses to cross
and recross this dark room, love's
floorshows and tricks having broken the bank,
the light bearing witness, a weight like smoke
having fallen away or been sidestepped.

10.

According to the majority of astronomers,
a constant breeze of dark matter
blows through us, the forever-dust of Creation,
the something we know nothing of, a glue-like
gravity of spiraling little-boy-lost bodies
tugged to and fro like the stars themselves.
A boy said once, in his sleep beside me,
with regard to the absolute tirelessness
of evil and death flying around out here—
I filled in the subject—*It stalks you.*
I know: it sounds too old for a child,
but he said it. And the total amount of light
in the room where he slept, sleeps yet,
they say speaks through a sulphurous haze
of secrets gravitating outward, ring-like,
a faint thunder rolling or the echoing
15-billion-year-old rumble of God
stomping the universe into shape.
Something dreamed of whispered beside you.
Something a boy says to no one in the night.

II.

They always look for it. Always.
They start from wanting to know
which road, which turn, how far, where,
to praying to any obvious marker to show them.
They have been hunting landmarks forever,
since that first looking up. This marker
is a poem against absolute closure, against lastness
and limit and death, against darkness
and getting and staying lost
while there is gas yet in the tank, fire
in the good engine that beats like a better heart.
The whole pentagonal starfish of its light
is a poem of arrivings and homecomings,
of places to come to just up the road.
That light falls on the free-flow of travelers.
I was in Nebraska, stopped by a rail line,
car after rocking car challenging the singings of geese,
one light on in the Badlands Motel,
when it came to me: there is forgiveness
in going. And if no forgiveness, going.

12.

Here between the sound of scythes
and noon-faced singing, another poor one
aches from bending while imagining
he were in a better, fairer country.
There is nothing fair or unfair about how light,
sinking along the honor prison of this row
and the next, inches past as if lost.
There is no loneliness in the single-mindedness
of leaves or a far-off dog barking,
but if he stops trying to shape the heart of him
he will cry. He may as well laugh and listen
to the deep drumming sound of bass notes
unreeling above the common grasses. But release
of breath isn't joy, and there's work to be done.
No, he may as well not dream or one of those
shaking shadows infinitely expanding will claim him
and all the regret he harvests here like wheat.
It isn't that a star above a road is monument
to nothing and no one, all he gets.
It isn't that we die, then it is.

13.

Either it's too much or truly magical, her turning
herself, but cartwheels have never looked like
something off the Playboy Channel, and she knows
she has your undivided attention. To call this
fantastic in the face of an eclipse's hesitating blush
would be to miss her eyes, older than motion,
and no one you know, loved or not,
ever laughed at the whole universe by doing what
makes perfect sense. Today, the unusual
is on schedule in the fortunate heavens overhead,
and the light looks like you're wearing Ray-Bans.
When she next extends, her closed fist of a sex
opens and the May-lit room holds its breath.
That pinkness deeper in bright as any sun, the push
and roll toward better days what the heart asks for.
If release of joy were light, you'd be bathed in it.
If love were this simple rotation, you'd turn and turn.
They say there is something rare in this presentation.
I say they should have someone so committed to delight.
It is just the two of you, and one hates getting dressed.

14.

A postcard of a cowboy neck-deep in snow:
The Trouble with a Short Horse in Montana—
I can hear a son's belly laugh above other voices.
We have been five days on the road, driving,
but he is glad again, and part of the world.
Someone has pumped a dollar's worth on the ground,
someone whose weariness announces
that something in us was not born to travel.
Talking with a woman on the pay phone in back
I let the field of flowers in a voice
become a name for where we are headed.
Perhaps the cowboy on the card is happy;
I suppose he is delighted to be outdoors
where all that whiteness is country he can travel through.
That scene is funny for the time it takes
to pay for a fill-up and Mountain Dews.
The boy leading the way is tired. Getting in,
on his side, I fix one of the cards
so he can glance up and smile, if he cares to,
the next however many miles.

Three

What Keats' Motives Were in Studying Medicine Are Not Known with Any Certainty

—Joseph Epstein. "The Medical Keats."

In the garden of the hospital
someone has paced a level, flat place
in grasses to the right of an entrance
resolving whether to take this or a less-
tracked course through the world. A row
of evergreen flash in light they belong to.
Keats attends to a cigar, firing the end
and describing a circle with a long lit match.
Torrents of smoke rage and disperse.

If ecstatic loss shivers the hand
trims a temporal artery, what then?
Shall the just-dead invite tentative
and exploratory flights into *materia medica*?
He may be recalling a cauterization:
banks of smoke spreading quick shadows
and a dark at the core. Poetry—
not the stench of wounds but the story

of all wounding—may have risen above a body
and into the bad air. Failing to know
everything might have called into question
where the lancet goes, and doesn't. Moreover,
there would have been the unfiltered agony
glazing a pair of eyes, the residue of death.
Beauty and death, is it even a contest? It is
the first anniversary of the day he penned

a sonnet, the poem as lifeless as market fish,
and he may be thinking of that short visit
to a house he seemed to belong in. As if
the better prescription for pain's cessation
were a deep swallowing, and words. He seems
to have a knack for staying with a thing, igniting
again the end of his cigar. Sighing at the truth
of a glow in a garden at noon only the beginning.

Shelley, after the Fatigue of an Unusually Long Walk

Imagine the poet had come in from the cold.
There is no winter there is no shiver like the one
won't be stopped inside except he plant himself
in front of a fireplace grate in a wingback chair,
both feet balancing on the wire fender, using it
like an ottoman—which he then overturns.

A dish of scalloped oysters "set within the fender,
to be kept hot for the famished wanderers"
flies up, lands on the chill fieldstone floor.

Has he not walked the steep and climbing path
where shapes loomed up in the lightlessness?
Is this not one who has capsized all the boats
of faith said to serve as conveyance and pathway
out of the dark country of the heart? In a year
he'll drown, be consigned to ash, but just now
he's got cinders and ash in his privileged hair.

Cinders and ash are nothing compared to a spray
of oyster-bits on a face appears to be counting
backward from one hundred in order not to laugh—
it's said he hates outbursts of levity more than
discussions of the menstrual cycles of certain bipeds.

So while he wears the ashes of the world that rise
to meet the ashes that fall—the oysters, too—
while he is the failed world, he is also its invocation
of nobility and amplitude. Shelley's face in firelight
is one of a good sport as others in the room
commence to laugh. Is this not one whose name
was writ, truly, in the fragrant scent of the sea?

The Beautiful Bird Revealing the Unknown to a Pair of Lovers

—Miro

Most of what is being said is lost, untranslatable,
But the rest is a great poem concerning
The huge debt of the hearers when this life
Taps out its code in a truth of self. If the bird

Is happy, its rhythmic singing a form of delight,
It doesn't show in the voicing of the thing—
If wingbeats and squawking lavished on the air
Can be called possessing a voice. The world

Has been changed, again, by a pair of lovers
Breaking off, listening to what dissolves
Across a too-solid sky the color of cornflowers.
Just now, the lovers have been marveling

At the plainer speech of a torn place below one wing.
They suspected; they knew nothing so miraculous
Could arrive having traveled the questionable country
Between without being changed. The bloody place

Proof the migration here isn't for the weak, the blood
Itself a story of distances. One of the lovers
Commences the business of the body; the other, transfixed
By the path of broken flight the bird reascends to.

Wild Turkeys, First Light

Brown-bodied, forward-thrusting,
in and out of a hillside's undergrowth,
they Egypt-walk: three strutters, after rain
syncopating to jazz from a kitchen window—
Carlos Santana's "Smooth"—as they inch
onto lawns to pluck first-shoot grasses.

Unhurried as heat, these have come down
past surveyors' stakes, past deer-printed mud,
between a wrecked ship of V-ed oaks initialed
by lovers. Having taken time into account,
they are timeless and present as in a drawing
by Audubon or a field guide: each blatant bird

emblematic of species. One displays, trilling
at tangential scent or threat. Maybe I seem
less predator than curiosity—white-robed,
behind a scrim of screen—but I'm watched
with more than passing interest. Maybe seeing
is believing to a turkey and it helps to be standing

as still as this rinsed-perfect summer air. Still,
my backlit shape must be more startling than God's:
They move off in a pattern resembling an S,
having surveiled the treeline like operatives
in service of whatever secret causes the biggest one
to shake as if flesh were burdensome in any light.

The Heron Tattoo

When I think of summer in Seattle, I think
of the tattoo parlor on Evergreen Way
in Everett, Washington, where Gloria Regalbuto
paid eighty dollars to have a Great Blue Heron
tattooed above her right breast, in four colors,
in answer to the tiger above my left breast.
I had never watched anyone being tattooed—
you can't really watch when they do it to you—
and I saw blood rise up from her, oxygenated,
bright, sulphur-colored, the never-completed blood
of her history and her apprenticeship to it.
She bled her mother's cruelty, the lesser bumps
of girlhood in Cleveland's Little Italy; she bled
her artist-father's successes, his failures, the art
of being able to talk Cleveland Browns football
from a hospital bed; she bled the surface of her face
changing from stunningly beautiful to just beautiful
to the uncertain nights lessening its best features;
she bled early menses, Catholic school, the lie
that pain is your ticket to Heaven. Then, it slowed;
the work was done—the rainbow-outline of body
restricted to shades of blue and deep-forest green,
the white top-beard of the bird's head, the legs
so identifiable as Bird as to be nearly a caricature.
When I think of love, being loved,
that's what I see, that bruise of a bird
standing on a lakeshore of flesh and seeing
itself and the world in eyes that happen to be
looking down, trying to disappear into another
whose blood's mirror is theirs and shining
with what is and isn't about to fly.

Because If Things Are Not Carefully Hidden

They shot the poet Federico Garcia Lorca
on a hillside flecked with olive trees,
in the company of a pair of bullfighters
and a schoolteacher. The sun had not risen
when Lorca and his companions heard the click of rifles.
Grave diggers, blackly obedient, went to work
in the pre-dawn, a lead man deciding depth
and the disposition of certain tree roots.

Years later, one of the diggers says the order
shivered the spine. He recalls the officer who
gave it chewed a reedy stalk of grass to pulp
and that the marathon work proceeded slowly:
"because if things are not carefully hidden..."
He says the last shovelfuls of Spanish earth
were lightstruck, there being no words for
Finish this grave that might as well be yours.

The Wreck of the Barbie Ferrari

—John Hiatt

Ken is standing in the mall parking lot
next to a carload of Mexicans when I get in
and take his place beside Barbie Millicent Roberts.
She wears something nautical, blue-white, designer,
those rocket breasts heartbreaking in profile.
We listen to jazz as she puts the machine
through its paces. She has a way with it,
but it is her nonchalance in traffic
says she is talented, blessed with good reflexes
and a tartarless smile. I put my tongue
in her perfect mouth at a four-way stop.
She says not to do that; I do it again.
It feels like I need to do *something* and,
besides, Ken did wave his model's wave
of acceptance resting on endless opportunity.
Either it's my imagination or she kisses back,
but we're kissing when she swerves
at 130 or more on a two-lane, pretending
she can drive and make love and downshift.
The girl has no idea of death, but she knows
some tricks as if avoidance of disaster
were a major and her Ivy League education
in becoming invisible a sort of secret shared.
We're clear. But then she parts her legs-by-Mattel
and her summer shorts ride up and she reaches
between the seat and her anatomical promise of
a WMD. I barely feel the impact, and I can tell you
that leaving this world is incremental, wishful thinking,
though it begins in terror and glancing upward.
When was the afternoon anything but a dull ache?

When did it begin to rain and you not notice
the blood river beside you smelled of setting gel?
She could use some help. We both could.

Shaved and Confused
or
Why a Woman Who Made Lord Byron a Gift of Her Pubic Hair Was Jealous of His Gift of £500 to Lady Falkland

She heard, from a friend, how he'd left the £500
in a teacup. She said she wanted to convert him

from his skepticism about the existence of God
or some Church of England facsimile thereof,

to save the soul of the poet from fiery judgment.
Damnation. I hear the blade of a straight razor

making its silvery way across flesh, its contours,
denuding the Boulevard of Dream as it crests

a nether ridge, a track his fingers are reported to
have taken. That scraping is no hymn of faith,

though it conjures what falls out of this world.
Which streets do we avoid, which bridges,

in the pursuit of pleasure? She signed the note
that accompanied her gift: *from your Wild Antelope.*

Hard Rain after Drought

Clouds flounce the distance above fields
and a day is as long as it always was,
except that grasses hunker down.
The grasses are nothing to me, I am
nothing to them, yet what swallows one
swallows the other and we are, together,
changed by that. Refusing to die
is the business of what lives, you bet.
And surely the upswirl of leaf-ends is closure,
a great novel in which the whale-god is spotted
on the horizon by the white of its spume,
luck and a future again harpooned. It may be
the fault of the rich few, or all of us, or none,
this change in the weather, but I'm thinking
that a downpour has a rightness to it borders
on the inscrutable and miraculous, especially
crossing a frontier of trees in slanting sheets
as if ruined fields again heavy with release
were destination the suddenly vaporous air found
not terribly concerned about where it was going.

Elvis on a Surfboard

Arrogance and stupidity are nothing special.
The false shore lies *You can go there.* Who cares
that he's had to diet the better part of 1961
to fit into these supposedly flattering trunks?

Who cares he's kept dozens waiting, cursing
in the California heat before air-conditioning?
The fake afternoon-at-the-beach backdrop
is for a postcard shoot. Before drifts of cloud,

if his body is making an invitation of itself
it does so knowing it's no big deal. Nor is
being king of a room of lamps. However,
there's the matter of the money, Samsonite

suitcases of it, and a collusion to letting oneself
be suckered out of bed, out of a sound sleep,
to be deposited into a limo and fed Dexedrine
en route to a blue-Hawaii fixed surfboard.

He waves one identifiable finger, grinds out
a life of movie-star pussy landed like trophy fish.
Out of sight, a fat bald man whispers, *You're*
the King—show some teeth: snarl. That's it. . .

He turns with the next direction, his job
to surf the high, white wave in the cup of light.
He will be hours, all day, skimming by trial
and terrible error a sea on sawhorses.

Jerry Lee Lewis at the Gates to Graceland

Jerry Lee says he showed the guard
his thoroughly pissed-off self, his .38 pistol.
With a tongue poised for preaching hellfire
and the fundamentalism of repeating one's own
name until it's a hymn, Jerry Lee
raved: *Elvis motherfucking Presley*
setting up there in that goddamned mansion,
pretending he's God... It was 3 A.M.
The guard hadn't heard "Whole Lotta Shakin'
Goin' On" or didn't care to hear, that late,
how Elvis was "a fat old dope addict."
Even if he was. The guy called the Memphis
police who said Elvis was as close to Jesus
Christ as they'd ever get, and besides
they were in the neighborhood. Jerry Lee
kept it up. Kept saying: *He dyes his hair*
like a goddamn woman until, finally,
he learned what I learned one winter
when I said I'd been to the Lorraine Motel
to see where Martin Luther King, Jr.
bled to death on a balcony—*You ain't been*
inside Graceland? You ain't seen nothin' then.
Jerry Lee got jail, a whack upside the head.
That was 1976, November, Presley ten months
from waking up dead in the john, nothing shaking.
Elvis, I'm not telling this to say anything about
you. But the world is abominably wrong:
you knew you weren't God, knew the sonofabitch
in the photos was you and them looking at you.
If art is—what?—an inarticulate speech it hurts
to deliver, worse not to, what exactly did you do?
Survived the beating they gave you for singing

the blues in a lusty-voiced Elvis-as-Elvis sideshow.
Survived them digging you up to take samples
and poke through your dead gut. Just to be sure.
Then putting you down in that second lowering
of the ropes by half a dozen locals. So you can't
blame Jerry Lee for wanting a piece of you.
And you can't blame the guy who drives the bus
from Graceland Plaza off Highway 51,
who says: *They say right there's where*
Jerry Lee Lewis parked his Lincoln Mark I
the night he came to get the King.
Came packing a Derringer pistol
because—well, no one but God knows why—
my guess is he just wanted in. Right
there. Some say he came to save Elvis.
Some say to kill him. You can't blame
the guy: he drives all day for
sixty-seven dollars and uniform money.
And tips. Whatever the people want...

Adult Films

That thrilling first double-feature at the World
unfolded labia the size of skyscrapers, men
with believe-it-or-not huge, circus penises.

I heard a rustle of belts behind, up the rows.
The X-rated truth of nineteen seventy-six
was that the woman beside me (my wife)

trembled and fidgeted, appalled and dizzied
as full-color anal and vaginal penetrations
rolled over her (and me) in dim movie light.

We lived in three small rooms. Ohio summers,
nights, you walked around in a baste of sweat
or went to theaters for the air conditioning;

we sat through violent swells of orgasm, heard
hours of soundtrack-passionate groanings (*Oh yes!*
Yes!) at the decibel level of jet aircraft. Leaving,

I drove. We had to pull over, park, get naked.
Years later, I laugh at the World's sea-smell
from decades of ejaculate loosed in the seats

in near-dark at the rear of the theater. I recall
having to fuck by a field starved for miracles,
how much in a hurry we were as we uncovered

there in the open. Afterwards, young,
spent, with every limb gone slack, we
held hands and entered again into traffic.

Second-billed to Simon & Garfunkel at Forest Hills, Jim Morrison Faces a Disinterested Audience

I've always thought of the Doors as the first punk band. . .
—Marilyn Manson

One assumes a backstage confrontation, a world
aswarm with hangers-on forgiven everything
atoned for by fellating the right minor god.

"Light My Fire" is no "Sounds of Silence" or "Mrs.
Robinson," but Morrison figures his leather pants
good for a few gasps. India-ink black, they cling,

a transparency like smoke over shadow. So what
if he's got the face of a sunken-cheeked angel—
a handful of front-row skeptics, unimpressed,

argue in loud whispers. They boo, and he spits
in their general direction, having downed two tabs
of Orange Sunshine, hours ago, at sound check.

His mind is a neon marquee of synaptic firings,
an echo of the cleanly detaching arc of his spit.
He waves to machinations overhead, the noises

of ropes, a pulley, repositioning a spotlight. Is it
too much to ask that he sing? The bright circle
he steps out of follows something muscular,

sly, ready to pounce. He's working the pants;
his hair wings wildly. Is it wrong, he wants
to rip the beautiful meat from their throats?

The Bodies of Bees

On the porch floor, members of a species
of honeybee hill up below an absence of screen
that keeps letting in the few who want to furniture
the houses of summer afternoons, ruminant.
They have been arriving and dropping for days,
adding up as if to finish a chore, weary travelers
in slant last light jays bruise around in.
The compass points of respective stingers
cancel out any indication of a true north
they'd have lifted off from, navigated toward,
and whatever stimuli of home teased antennae
abstracted the wet and flowering distances between
as a single idea variously received.
Nothing to be done but to grab a broom
and make the bristles hiss like falling water
we barely hear in the crowning of brightest moon.
There is a peppery scent to the weight of these;
they roll darkly, easily, losers in the war
for territory and warmth in the amoral moment.
As many blue flies as bees, as many scrim-winged
anopheles mosquitoes as broad-backed horseflies.
Of all the insects in this story of place
why'd these end up here?
The value of working out one's own salvation
in meeting and passing another so engaged
a shadow on a porch shiny with moonlight
and the screened quiet where you're standing
recalling their many voices come back now—
the depth of the world reducible to broom sounds,
the underside of the buzz beneath any particular hour
a pair of hard taps to disengage the last to go.

On the Way to a Bob Dylan Concert

In Milwaukee, a one-eyed Kuwaiti cab driver
brakes, accelerates, disparaging American women,
women in general, and Wisconsin Avenue.
The cabby's lack of oneness with the Universe
is consigned to a rear-view mirror dreamcatcher
whose center fills with a Kerry-for-President button.
He has a preoccupation with periods, this immigrant-
Arab who confesses to trying his hand at stand-up.
"Divorce judges are most frightening," he riffs,

"if they're on the rag at the same time as her lawyer."
He's captaining a blue boat of a Chevy Biscayne
passengered by a pair of South African women,
a Sicilian-American woman (my wife) and me.
It's clear the tip will suffer, facial disfigurations
having failed to invoke pity. What's to be done
from a backseat, enroute to the Eagles Ballroom,
except to keep my own male rhetoric divorced
from soft-pedaling the language of misogyny?

Then, too, there is this joy in going to hear Dylan
sing *She aches just like a woman* in a voice as shaky
as the proposition men ever understand women.
I focus on the rocking mandala and Kerry button
before a dashboard's numerical red drum-tick.
I learned the power of silence from a woman
might just as easily have said, *Pull over, jerk.*
A swath of red behind the figure on the button
editions anticipation, the new, and blood.

for Denise Smith

Four

Motorcade

Four-positioned American flags, 48-starred,
flap in the air before and behind my father's
'56 Cadillac DeVille, snap from the big chrome lip
of a front grille. The road ahead
is a line of like-minded Kentucky veterans
motorcading to Frankfort to tell Bert Combs,
Republican governor, that just because the only work
is in Ohio, nothing changes the fact
the State of Kentucky owes its veterans *something*.

We have the PA system. A bank of tubes blooms
to life on the floor between the seats—a voice,
my father's, booms out how we're almost there.
Nettie, my mother, brushes my short hair. Says
we'll be stopping for cheeseburgers and Co-colas.
We're following this red Merc with black tailfins
I bet would be boring to God after a while.
My father won't tell us, for years yet, what he's seen
in the service of this his country. If there are words,
then they're barked-out directions, orders

to the other cars, his big voice otherworldly and
traveling now alongside the motorcade,
in the passing lane of this brand-new interstate.
Glassed in this way, for all I know at 5, we're
on our way to Alabama and a civil rights march,
but there are no black faces in the cars
that have crossed again into Kentucky, their homeland,
to get what's theirs. There was the guy with hooks
for hands who could drive a car, his luminous face
nothing to do with loss. And the soon-to-be-judge lawyer
from Dayton who might as well have been Abraham Lincoln.

And, of course, they got their money. Every cent.
I got this memory of my father that will not die.
He's the voice shouts to the world, *You owe me money!*
when all Bert Combs needed was the redneck equivalent
of Martin Luther King, Jr. calling him "a son-of-a-bitch
Republican" at noon on the capitol steps. Whoever
he saw my father to be, standing on the hood of a Cadillac,
breezes blowing his Kentucky Colonel necktie to one side
in the middle of the tangle of cars below, he went
down. To shake hands and promise him anything.

Roy's Shell, 1962

Father, in the stock room of your filling station
the new hire talked about missiles and women.
A scallop-shaped Timex purled out a surf of light
the color of lemonskins; the sweep second-hand
ticked blackly across a face and numerals. Not
restocking oil and wiper blades on the pump islands,
that was more than a bad thing, cause for firing,
but milling around while war loomed was different
since Dayton's air force base was a first-strike target
in any nuclear exchange. That's what they called it,
an exchange. Which prompted the new mechanic
to use Armageddon as a metaphor for a break-up
with an eager brown-eyed woman whose departure
left him feeling like his heart was scorched earth.
He was trying to tell his second-shift fellow workers
about the twentieth-century A.D. and who it was
dared say love has a wretched shape sometimes
and lovers a tendency to misstep. The headlines
all said we were goners, to be made immaterial,
together, pump-bell anointings of commerce
bled as silent as a fallout shelter. All of Kettering
was holding its breath anyway, so what if misrule
began with a handful of men grandly present
in the back room of a service station? So what
if a boy was hearing what he had always heard
but more acutely because it was what he'd miss?
If Fidel Castro didn't care anymore about women
or what happens in a country where lies have a life
and afterlife, we'd be toast by week's end. The guy
talking about his lost love knew this, must have.
Why else would words so freight the gasoline-air
heavy already with an anthem of bells and engines?

Hillbilly Music

The night I complained in the Confederate gallery
of the Ryman Auditorium in Nashville, Tennessee
my father said, *That's Ernest Tubb,*
that's Hank Snow. The church-pew seats
weren't comfortable in 1969; there was no
air conditioning and you fanned yourself
with programs and funeral home fans.
Eddy Arnold sang "Cattle Call," yodeling

to Chet Atkins' guitar accompaniment.
A woman in a cowgirl skirt and boots
swayed at a stand-up microphone; she
was doing her best Patsy Cline. My mother
asked my father, *You had enough, Roy?*
It was June, sweltering hot, but my father
had listened to the Opry on a Zenith Trans-
Oceanic every Saturday night since Korea,

and he wasn't in a hurry to collect us
for the drive back to the motel. He'd taken
all the shit he wanted about hillbilly music;
he told my mother, *After Roger Miller. Here's*
five bucks, Nettie. Buy the boy a Co-Cola.
She ushered me through a sea of applause—
if I close my eyes, I hear a shudder of pleasure—
out, into the lobby where the big doors let in

a breeze, Tennessee summer. Behind us,
inside, they were dreaming out loud. Inside,
it was all right to talk with the drawl and hoot
and bathe in a faith light of rank sweat.
Inside, he worshipped the oceanic emptiness

of growing up dirt-poor. We waited. Then
my mother checked her big Tammy Wynette hair
in the glass of a storefront, hailed a taxi.

for Charles Wyatt

Speaking with a Single Tongue

I.

First the word Jesus, the tongue
still thick with stresses and repetition,
then Kentucky, the K popping out crisply.
She's never heard it like that before,
she's Catholic and among Pentecostals.
Adelay's 13 or 14. All that talk of hellfire
and eternal damnation hits home
like the deep, rattling cough of a father
come in from a double shift at Elkhorn Coal.
Something stubborn in her wants to cry out
how this isn't what she'd prayed for,
but she's respectful before the framed Christ
hanging from baling wire on the canvas tentside,
the dead-and-risen Savior looking like a tormented
Ricky Nelson. Like radio baseball, letter perfect,
that's how she sounds to herself, like the words
she knows in her own way aren't working. Like
the Holy Ghost has it in for stutterers.
There are 15 or 20 crows in the front yard
speaking with a single tongue, cacophonous,
paying her no mind as she walks in from the tent meeting
and Reverend Ray MacFall's plain, open palm
across her child mouth's outline. The news
has beat her home, and neighbors trickle in
to hear proof, in 1960, of miracles and wonders.
But she's not talking. She doesn't want to, but then
words come rushing out in the Saturday afternoon light,
every clipped syllable unrepeatably mending something,
something mournful if not joyous, young-in-Christ
if not holy.

2.

When Adelay takes up with the Preston boy
from over Big Stone Gap, it starts—
her stretching certain words like *geese* or *wings*
until you can make out the cadences of wingbeats,
raucous bodies flying north-to-south in V's
the hour before or just after sunset.
They call it backsliding, but she can hear
Bobby Preston's sweet quickening breathing
pound an awful lot like she remembers
the sewing factory that first hour's first minutes
when life is noise, machine pedals
stitching silence to morning like the air itself
were clothing. If this is backsliding, sin,
it wears white bucks and kisses like God Himself
after the Powell Valley High School band
rises in the pine bleachers at a touchdown
to play a raspy "Great Balls of Fire."

3.

A natural gas company called Equitable
Resources Exploration tried to buy this hillside,
the home place. Fifteen women
named Wright linked themselves before bulldozers,
their broad arms folding back on each other
like ribbon candy. They stopped them, big oaks
leafing now above these houses where
one of their own has been chosen
to remind us what Heaven wants Heaven gets.
The girl's got her hands folded in her lap.
The men laugh easily in the kitchen.
They turn back to their pound cake and coffee.
One man named Mullins is talking of inching his way
to the mouth of the mine last year
after an explosion. He says there were stars,
or darknesses would have all looked the same.

4.

She doesn't know where he is
but the tires of Mopar Plymouths, Fords,
chirp boyish joys up and down
narrow routes that fall under the high stars,
along mountainsides, like Christmas ribbon.
She waits, learns to sit quietly
and watch for headlight-glow, outrageously white,
or listen for the gravel note of his coming.
For hours, only the bad-picture Motorola
and deep currents of poor reception
settle into *Maverick.* She is waiting
for a chance not to speak of God's glory
and yet still be heard. And if he comes at all
it will be too late to do anything
but sit on the porch and witness moonlight's
infinitely gentle impact on floor boards
older than God. Saying what?
Not saying. That would be enough.

5.

After, Adelay looks out
at morning—down, onto a garden
plowed by hand and letting the tired horse
have a chew of Red Man when he's through.
There are nine houses, all of them family.
In one, a fire is banked to a blaze
by hands that make music. In another,
the first slap of the day reminds a woman
it isn't so much hard as her life
in these hills where healing is brief,
God help us all.

for David Baker

The Morning After the Running of the 116th Kentucky Derby

In the short hall of the slave house
ten dozen calla lilies in vases.
The lilies sweeten the heavy Bourbon County air,
add an apple-rosiness and stark white trumpeting
the Sunday after Unbridled, teasing the have-nots,
took a good field of thoroughbreds
by six lengths and then some. A woman

in a simple white robe of terry cloth
is on her way to the kitchen. In a ritual,
she commences closing the robe around her
on this her thirty-fifth birthday. She stops
by a black phone, presses the numbers. Talks
to the friend whose generosity blooms in tears.

She's a thin woman, barely here, ready to bolt
for any better place. She talks like it's talk
keeps the lie of most of life from overhearing
and daring us to do better, if ever
we really meant to live at all.

Now she's lighting a cigarette, inhaling
with that I-will-outlast-the-elms casting-off
of mere mortality. This one will live forever
until the call ends and she must go about
that other business the course of which never yet
ran smooth. There's a horse she'll ride, in every way

the horse's body responding, drinking light.
But she's hours from that and the small hands
of the leaves drip rain this May morning.
The long windows say only *Get going, get going.*

Row Houses

On the other side of this two-lane Kentucky state route
they're stopping, out of respect. Not just slowing down.
You really can't lose the story of this place, this day,
once you understand the stunned-deer look in the eyes
and on the faces of soaked-through local kids on bicycles.
At least there's wealth in that light, long stretches
where death isn't just news but part of all that talk talk

of resurrection. Lies like that make an abstract, walking-
naked sound like rain and radial tires in the unbusy afternoon.
You want daylight not to harbor even one well-intentioned remark
about there being a God who knows there are row houses
and an unstoppable fading. Jesus, we're always dying.
The better case to be made is for a deity forgets
that to love any part of the world is miracle, and enough.

If there is something one of these houses holds back
it's that free enterprise ends here, at heart a boast:
hundred-year-old collapsing towns, hill-fenced,
the shuddering junk wood of insufficiency. On the curving
cold-shouldered road we're driving past these
and the soul's other load of coal smoke. Yellow scarves of it.
No one can tell you anything new about coal smoke.

Light as Story

A half moon bright as the windows of a lit church
and the shining teeth of standing-dead hardwoods

are *1961*: the white-on-navy rolled leather interior
of my father's blue '56 Coupe DeVille, plastic-canary

pastel yellow of Mother's '58 Sedan DeVille: light
that means it's not night forever, light as story.

My parents were flush that year: two Cadillacs
and the crooner Perry Como and *The Wizard of Oz*

on the color Zenith TV my father won in a raffle,
Childhood's daily-levitating body of dreams

and the hole in the air where the Impossible goes
anything but Ohio-drab black-and-white. Sure,

they had it made. All right, they blew it on lawyers
and a divorce before the year was out. So what.

Though it flickered, there was all this light—
streetlights, the Shell sign of my father's station,

summer lightning, the immense truths of Dayton
where the beginning of the world came on streets

named for tribes of defeated and dead Indians.
If I should move from this doorway, it's gone;

if I could take it inside and hand it to someone
as a thing to be placed in safe keeping, I would.

My Name Is Bentley

after Martin Espada

Bentley: the word for meadow in Chaucerian English
signifying cleared spaces, open-air cathedrals of thorns,
name for untrammeled acres thick with brambles and
spiny starts watered by rivers of run-off and snowmelt,
or the serviceable-for-a-border little dark-soiled places
and unambiguously black aftermaths of cleansing fire.

Bentley: the car of Queen and Beatle, expensive
and funereal, road tested by Congolese chauffeurs
on their nights and days off, plush reliable machines
for the Super Rich whose vanity falls back at no god
or sermon on the virtues of beneficence, spoked wheels
for the thoroughfares of Europe and North America.

Bentley: meadow of Suffering's end, undeeded paradise
of those who swear at a recalcitrant God for practice;
teachers of workers and freed slaves and immigrants;
gamblers and wastrels and drunks whose unquiet deaths
struck no bell-brass of freedom as they succumbed;
all accomplished at the study of the maps of hard hands.

Bentley: cousin to the horse, carrier of burden and saddle
for a master knows the cinch at the belly of the beast,
cousin to mules hitched to loader cars and darknesses
cut into the bowels of mountains, kin to the flinching
at harsh words because there's that remembered life,
family name for frontier crossers swindled yet again.

Bentley: mothers to bastard sons who would love
their lives, with or without a father, with or without
even a mother-madwoman to break again the heart,
sisters to washing women with .45's in apron pockets
or within reach, loaded, covered over with dry leaves
in laurel thickets where they had been raped already.

Bentley: a horse's Appalachian rider-cargo doctoring
from row house to row house on moonless nights
when some blink of starlight from a shard of Mason jar
drew the animal on, this before talk of a proletariat's
early death at the hands of mine bosses who order, *You're*
in hell when I say you're in hell, now get to work.

The doctor died chasing death from the beds of the poor
in a gift-Cadillac exhaustion aimed at last at an abutment—
so the provenance of sorrow in the faces in photographs
whispers our name, commands me to taste its salt: Bentley.

Appalachian Cooking for Two

If there are requests for ingredients, they're shouts
and threats said Southern—nothing like cooperation
exists without all that's fairly bartered, and sex—
he'll tell her how to do it, how Dear Mother did it,
yet when skillets of corn bread emerge from heat,
it's her hand in the towel, the no-surprise burn
all hers. If words are a meal, they're also a hunger.

He sees sacrifice in her face, hates that they've set
a table to be overturned and righted once more
as if there is being uncared for and something
much worse. To make a meal according to no recipe,
rinse each bean till it is both a small tear and weeps.
For what's true in spite of us and as a consequence
of ordinary heartbreak having become bodied.

My Hands Enter Dirt Easily, a Premonition

—Bob Hicok

Baptist theologians would say my grandmother B.
wouldn't have cared for words like *righteous*
or concepts of faith like *washed in the blood* or *redemption.*
She knew the world as entitlement. Never mind

"visits" to a sanitarium or her rage at men: they say
she ran my father's father to higher ground, treed him,
with a .45 she was (the story goes) reloading when arrested.
The story of an egg route is apocryphal, most likely,

but involves a Model A with rumble seat, harsh parents,
a married man with children whose combed-perfect hair
said there is no perfect life only this one in which
certain distant and less distant birdsongs voice courtship.

After shock treatments, after whole days in restraints,
does God know what's set in motion has rolled over us?
She said she wished death would take her. Once
she said it as if it could be a windfall, an almost song

from whichever muscular throat shivers a howl. We
buried her on a January-frozen hillside above and
overlooking a convenience store. It was below zero,
windy, and I hurried to toss in my handful of earth.

The Beasts of the Fields

In the east this morning, too generous as usual
and risen as from a blue heaven of roof,
                    the sun dumped its new load of old light

onto the bodies of running horses. Then
          across already-trampled timothy
                    and wind-ticking grasses, alfalfa;

everything alive and hard-used in the fields
          refashioned, made flat as a hand: to slap
awake the sleepy face of the world.

I know this isn't what happens most days
          –or is it? There is no telling
                    what suppleness of form

another hour of breath will take. Who doesn't
          want daybreak to pour itself like smoke
                    or reasonably pure water, out,

the grazed way to and from the gate flaming with dew?
Isn't it the case—and when dark comes early—
                    that this found shape is what we are?

Red Scarf

It is 1929, the year of the Great Stock Market Crash.
My great-grandmother leaves the Bank of Fleming
with an apron full of currency. The other depositors
watch the bank's president step to long wood-and-glass doors
and pull down a roll-up blind, turn the CLOSED sign
streetward, that fragile instant become memory and proof
there is nothing to trust in this world. She walks
up a street fleshed with a weight of faces.
Strangely enough, a bloom of dust precedes her,
the ancient door-hinge of aroused interest
singing open and banging shut at her back.
She's having trouble with the contents of the apron,
a coin or two dropped dully, positing nothing.
Her neighbors have decided it is easier to look than not;
then again, they have always known who among them,
come hell or high water, would swallow the last bite
of the bounty of a place. She has a ways to go, keeps going,
and with both hands clamped with righteous ownership
on the lap-cargo of the apron. Strands of hair
work loose from a red scarf, shine resolutely. She
doesn't want squat to do with the day's last hours
in the town her father's father built, bare-handed,
yanking compliance and concession from Nature.
My father knows this story like the drifting smells
of suppers of soup beans and cornbread. Once
he said it and sloshed an extra jigger of whiskey
into a glass of crushed ice, the ice cracking
with sudden warmth after so much cold.
You need to understand men who understand women
who will break the bank because it's theirs, how
it really is mixed up with the dead and what
they carry to us like a small hoarded fortune
wants to work itself loose with every step.

Kitchen

The Osborne Brothers used to meet every so often
in the kitchen of our house on Comanche Drive
to play "Ruby"—Sonny, who played banjo,
and his brother Bobby who could be
counted on to bring his mandolin; and Benny
who dated May, my mother's best friend,
and bedded down on our sofa once or twice
over my mother's protests; and May
who wanted Benny more than anything; and
my mother who wanted them to keep it down
because it was after midnight. That year

my mother and May machine-cut sealant strips
for General Motors cars and trucks at Inland
Manufacturing. I remember my grandmother Potter
would leave dinner for both women—pinto beans,
cornbread, onion slices—on the white Westinghouse
stove: plates covered bowls of fried apples, ham,
ham gravy, grits, green beans. In Ohio in 1963,

factory work was the only work a woman could get
that paid, which was how my mother knew May
who knew everyone. They brought the Osborne Brothers
and Benny Birchfield home from the White Sands nightclub
to eat my granny's soup beans and cornbread
and play music until Granny was shaken from sleep
by either Sonny or Bobby or Benny cutting loose
or May or my mother laughing too loudly or harmonizing
until they forgot Dayton, Inland, the hour, my
absent father who was why my mother worked.
Life is exhumed through music like that.
If I woke I saw through a haze of cigarette smoke

my mother or May look in my direction, eventually,
as if to say, Yes, you should hear this…

The hill on Comanche Drive was not always level
at the top. Just before my father left, he had it
bulldozed, saying that he'd build a bomb shelter
and better house higher up on the cleared place.
They uncovered a graveyard in the bulldozing,
the dozer driver refused to finish, and so
my father said the spot was cursed ground and
rolled three gravestones down the hill—to a place
below the window over the kitchen sink. He set
his garbage cans on the marble markers, though
you could still read the names and dates on them.

From the kitchen those nights the Osborne Brothers
(and Benny Birchfield) played you could read the stones:
all you had to do was to climb up, onto the sink, sit—
your back to the goings-on—turn and look down
into the dark. The light was that bright
from the kitchen or maybe it was moonglow
poured down upon the hill's one lighted house.

Now, when I hear "Rocky Top" or "Georgia Moon,"
Sonny and Bobby, maybe Benny (though he left May
and the Osborne Brothers soon after), I scent
pinto beans, onions. I see my young mother's
face through cigarette smoke. I think, as I turn
upon my high perch at the sink and catch
the marblelight of names, *Who are these strangers?*

Air Freight

They air freighted my grandmother Bentley,
cardboard-cartoned and in death clothes,
to Bristol, Tennessee from Orlando, Florida.

The poor soul escaped cremation by an hour.
Ambulanced to an airport at night, they dollied
and dragged her into a plane's underbelly—

to ride beside luggage, the next day's mail—
so we could stand over her embalmed body
with its summoning and white-haired head

on a neck-pillow of rough pine. The wood,
its unpretentious and grave placement, siphoned off
the niceties about the natural end of loving

anything. And it broke my father's heart,
the way her head rested at last, having traveled
the precincts of the covert dark for a fee.

He stood by her in a fan of granular light,
fussing with an implacable lock of hair and the details
of what she couldn't afford, wouldn't want

at any price. How like herself she was—
valiantly small, nothing like laugh lines anywhere
on that face of hers—napping, as usual,

through inevitable, necessary negotiations
at the end of which my father waved off all talk
and turned his back and walked to a window.

All This and Hell to Look Forward to

The voice of Billy Graham, its Southern-
accented breathiness and certainty, its freight
of pronouncements about death and afterlife,
sin and redemption, broke my grandmother down
in the living room of our house on Comanche Drive.
Ricky David Ozzie and Harriet, Lucy and Ricky
and Little Ricky, the way things made sense then—
you can't imagine living through it—even the bagger
at the A&P sure about the Machine Gun of God
telling Yankee Stadium how Hell was a place
with an address as real as Central Park West,
hotter than adolescent first kisses. I know,
but that voice sent her into fits of *Praise Jesus!*
and *My Sweet Savior!* until I wanted to run.
He was her Elvis, I guess, but I couldn't wait
for him to get to the part where he prays
and they voice-over his face and roll credits
and let TV take us somewhere as familiar, in 1961,
as Rod Serling's *Twilight Zone.* So what
if two-thirds of Yankee Stadium accepted Christ,
I didn't want to hear another Amen.
I wanted to watch anything else, anything—
even *The Lawrence Welk Show,* though
there it was again: that heart brimming over
with the Gospel According to Protestantism,
its evasions and daily banalities a fat worm
devouring the apple of the world from the inside.
I wanted delivered from her sorrowful rocking
in her housedress, her hair a mouse-gray cascade,
the thrust-and-retreat motion faith, all right,
as she kept on raising her thin arms ceilingward—
I was a kid, for Godssakes; she was scaring me.

She believed every black-and-white word
out of Billy Graham's mouth. Time isn't salvation.
Lost is something you don't get used to.
I want saved, too. I wanted to say, *Make it stop.*
I didn't then, and she's dead: Make it stop.

The Other Pile

And here comes the angel with her drum
and wings. Some wings.
—Charles Wright

After the phone call
testified to your abandonment of the body,
a lucky guy at last to have gone on
easily and without warning, before the Big Snow
you wanted to blanket your life in Ohio just once,
before that snow fell—*Asshole-deep,* you'd have said—
before that further dissipation of middle age
and your share of collapses, did you know
I reread that story of yours about Bob?
It's May, in the story, and you've got Bob perched
in a blue Ford front-end loader with a pile
of manure to spread. The stuff is so bad,
whoever owns the place has waited so long
into spring to move it, that Bob's getting double time
for as long as it takes. You've got maggots
white and wriggling, unhoused; you've got poor Bob
retching his guts out after the first full pass.
Anyway, you were saying this whole thing stinks
and double time won't touch it, and careful or not
we come away with the worst of it all over us.

When I was a kid, I had a GI Joe
with a makeshift Superman suit under his fatigues.
In the course of play his uniform could—*tada!*—
fall away and he wasn't just some foot soldier
to be spent at the whim of his superiors
according to the requirements of Mission—
as if there could be a Superman beneath the wardrobe

of any one of us. Though my aunt Peg
who did the sewing didn't do snaps very well,

it didn't matter GI Joe was stuck with Superman duds.
I wanted him invulnerable, whether or not he could ever
move his pretend bowels or take a pretend piss.
Immortals don't need to let it out like that, I figured.
Later my aunt told me about Jesus being, becoming,
a kind of Superman after he rose from the dead,
graveclothes flapping in the breezes of an Easter dawn,
savior to the world of us measly GI Joes.
I told her I could use a cape from something
other than corduroy. A redder scrap S this time, too.

I am so happy for you, Christopher.
The heart it would take x-ray vision to watch beat
slowed in your white sleep, stopped altogether—*tada!*—
before you could even raise yourself. For sure,
it's that we're one breath above a stinking shitpile
short of a good day, but you know now
whether there are angels, supermen, risen Jesuses,
and you at least left us Bob in the front-end loader
telling us how the trick is (and it isn't much of a trick)
to keep the wind at our back.

It's snowing, and you know what?
If you venture out into it—maybe you used to—
and look straight up, through the wet, at stars or nothing,
the naked skin of the face will catch
and melt handfuls of what's falling
in startling 3-D lifelike action, catch it
as if the miraculous could pile up by pure chance

before it is itself changed, added to,
held up to Krypton or New Jerusalem, S's of tears
made to river every curved and exposed inch.

for Christopher Zenowich

Roy Bentley has published two books of poems—*Boy in a Boat* (University of Alabama Press, 1986) and *Any One Man* (Bottom Dog Books, 1992)—and four chapbooks: *The Way into Town* (Signpost Press, 1984), *The Edge of Heaven* (Bottom Dog Books, 1987), *Reparation* (Puddinghouse Books, 2001) and *Greatest Hits, 1982-2001* (Puddinghouse Books, 2002). A six-time winner of the Ohio Arts Council Individual Artist Fellowship award, he is also the recipient of a National Endowment for the Arts Individual Artist fellowship in poetry. His work has appeared in the *Southern Review, Pleiades, Sou'wester, North American Review, Shenandoah, New Virginia Quarterly, The Journal* and elsewhere. He lives in Stuart, Florida.

The White Pine Press Poetry Prize

Vol 11 *The Trouble with a Short Horse in Montana* by Roy Bentley
Selected by John Brandi

Vol. 10 *The Precarious Rhetoric of Angels* by George Looney
Selected by Nin Andrews

Vol. 9 *The Burning Point* by Frances Richey
Selected by Stephen Corey

Vol. 8 *Watching Cartoons Before Attending A Funeral*
by John Surowiecki
Selected by C.D. Wright

Vol. 7 *My Father Sings, To My Embarrassment* by Sandra Castillo
Selected by Cornelius Eady

Vol. 6 *If Not For These Wrinkles of Darkness* by Stephen Frech
Selected by Pattiann Rogers

Vol. 5 *Trouble in History* by David Keller
Selected by Pablo Medina

Vol. 4 *Winged Insects* by Joel Long
Selected by Jane Hirshfield

Vol.3 *A Gathering of Mother Tongues* by Jacqueline Joan Johnson
Selected by Maurice Kenny

Vo. 2 *Bodily Course* by Deborah Gorlin
Selected by Mekeel McBride

Vol. 1 *Zoo & Cathedral* by Nancy Johnson
Selected by David St. John